Praise for *Swing Thoughts*

"David has cleverly taken thoughts we apply to an aspect of our lives many men spend too much time thinking about … and applied them to an area many don't spend enough time thinking about. Perhaps the simple applications he provides will help us to get our thought lives in proper balance."

*David Cardenas, Partner, Olympus Partners*

"Golf, like faith, is a life-long game that requires patience, focus, commitment, practice and . . . the hardest part . . . relaxation. After accumulating all life's lessons, you ultimately need to let the muscle memory take over. David Felts' wonderful and concise book gives us a few simple swing thoughts for how to live a life filled with faith. He then encourages us to just clear our minds. And to swing."

*Bill Antholis, Managing Director, the Brookings Institution*

"*Swing Thoughts* is simply outstanding. I pray that it will go viral more quickly than we "average golfers" can possibly imagine. There are billions of duffers on our rock who will be inspired and encouraged by reading it and sharing it with their foursomes."

*Bert Smith, Executive Director,*
*Prison Entrepreneurship Program*

"David Felts has figured out the spiritual intersection of the games of golf and life. After reading his book, I'm quite certain that you will see some parallels that help you both on and off the course."

*David Ingram, Chairman and President,*
*Ingram Entertainment Inc.*

"*Swing Thoughts* is as important to have close at hand in life, as a yardage book is on the golf course. I have witnessed David's passion to love and serve others well. His wisdom from experience is captured in these short devotions, each one packing a powerful life application that promises much fruit when put into action."

*Stanton Lanier, Pianist of Peace*

"The game of golf is richly entertaining to play and to watch. After reading *Swing Thoughts,* I will never see the game the same again. Seeing the game through the lens of this book goes from entertaining to life changing. Profound and clever insights connected to common occurrences. Illustrations that really stick with you. This book will improve the most important game any of us play . . . the game of life!!! The Bible tells us that we must constantly renew our minds . . . *Swing Thoughts* will do just that—in a way that will improve your life!!!"

*David Salyers, Vice President Marketing, Chick-fil-A, Inc.; co-author,* Remarkable!

"*Swing Thoughts* may or may not improve my golf game. I'm a duffer at best! But for sure my faith walk has encountered 'swing thoughts' that have impacted the way I will live my life going forward. On and off the course."

*Dennis Worden, Worden Associates, Editor/Publisher of* The Chase

"I love David Felts and his new book. You will be blessed to read and take to heart his points of instruction and inspiration. Enjoy!"

*Boyd Bailey, Co-founder, CEO, Ministry Ventures; Founder, President, Wisdom Hunters*

"From the authentic heart of a mature follower of Jesus, this little book can bring God's technicolor to what can be an intense black and white game. I'll give *Swing Thoughts* to every golfer I know!"

*Regi Campbell, Entrepreneur, Founder of Radical Mentoring, and author of* About My Father's Business *and* Mentor like Jesus *(www.radicalmentoring.com)*

"I didn't really know golf until the last tour of my Air Force career. As commander of Nellis Air Force Base, Nevada, I played our base course frequently with a group of retired Airmen—and David's *Swing Thoughts* encapsulate most of what I learned about companionship and leadership in 24+ years as a fighter pilot, commander, and average golfer. What a great, quick read for anyone looking to refocus their game and their life."

*Col (ret) David Belote, former commander of Nellis Air Force Base, NV*

"In golf, and in our journeys of faith, there are transcendent moments of triumph, and also of abject failure. David's simple words of wisdom encourage us to keep swinging, and to enjoy the beauty of the round, and of life!"

*Dave Stockert, Chief Executive Officer, Post Properties*

# Swing Thoughts

SIMPLE OBSERVATIONS TO
IMPROVE OUR CHRISTIAN LIVES . . .

AND MAYBE EVEN
OUR GOLF GAMES

David M. Felts

First Edition Printed, 2013

ISBN: 978-0-9893674-0-0

Library of Congress Control Number: 2013908140

Printed in the United States of America by Booklogix, Alpharetta, Georgia

This book may be purchased in bulk for educational, business, fundraising or sales promotional use. For information please contact:
**David M. Felts, david@swingthoughtsbook.com**

Cover and interior layout design by: Vanessa Lowry

THE HOLY BIBLE, NEW INTERNATIONAL VERSION®, NIV® Copyright © 1973, 1978, 1984, 2011 by Biblica, Inc.™ Used by permission. All rights reserved worldwide.

# Dedication

Please allow me a moment to dedicate this book to those around me who have significantly impacted my life and influenced my faith journey. To my wife and soul-mate Jill, who has been such an encourager and whose own faith journey has served to light the path for me. To my awesome daughters Jessica and Shannon, whose life energy and faith are an example to their father. To my parents, who nurtured me and loved me and provided me many opportunities. And to the countless men of faith ... in church, in business and particularly within the Souly Business men's retreat ministry . . . who helped me make some progress in my own faith journey by serving in their own unique ways as living witnesses to the abundant life in Christ.

# Table of Contents

# Preface

*"Swing Thoughts"* are those simple thoughts golfers focus upon as they set-up to hit a particular shot. Maybe it's a reminder to focus on hand-alignment; or to take the club back smoothly; or to rotate your hips; or to keep your head down. It may, in fact, be the thought to clear your mind of any thoughts at all.

This "swing thought" represents that single, over-riding thought that a player believes should have the most influence on the outcome of that particular shot, at that particular point in time. Titling this book *Swing Thoughts* seemed appropriate.

For you see, the original inspiration for this book occurred on a Saturday around midnight, when it first dawned on me that I was scheduled to teach a class at my church the next morning. I quickly reviewed a few Christian-related books, and found nothing particularly inspiring. At the point of minor panic, a stream of observations entered my mind regarding some inter-esting relationships between our Christian faith journey . . . and the game of golf. One thought followed another in fairly rapid succession, and soon I had a collection of scribbled notes that would become the basis for my one hour lesson. Many of the chapters in this book are direct descendants of those original notes.

I should confess to you now, I am a pretty "average golfer." I have played for many years, enjoy the game, and know more about what I "should" do than I can consistently put into practice. (The same can be said of my personal faith journey.) I regularly shoot in the 90s, with the occasional rounds of a low 100 and mid-80s. My friends may think this characterization of my golf game is quite charitable.

My scoring is an eclectic combination of moments of brilliance (pars and a few birdies), and "snow men" (8s)—where I hit the ball out of bounds or in the water. (The same can be said of my personal faith journey.) Mine is a volatile game; one in which within any four-some I am equally likely to hit the best shot, or the worst.

Throughout *Swing Thoughts*, I employ the game of golf in an overall metaphor as it relates to our Christian lives. The "ball" may be that circumstance or need we face at the moment. The "swing" is taking some action as a Christian. The "course" represents the circumstances of our lives. I trust other examples will be self-evident.

My intention is that *Swing Thoughts* will illustrate the interesting connectedness between the game of golf and our faith journey.

Grace and Peace, David Felts

# Acknowledgements

There are many folks who have helped this "average golfer" and "finance guy" to get *Swing Thoughts* ready for launch. I want to thank my wife Jill and daughters for reading early versions repeatedly, and for such good suggestions and edits. Further, I need to thank Jill for pushing me forward on this project. As we got closer, I want to thank Dennis Worden for his encouragement and introduction to Anne Alexander (Word Wise LLC), who gave a professional editing scrub. Then my wife introduced me to Vanessa Lowry, who took the reins and brought *Swing Thoughts* to life with cover design, layout, production advice and contacts. Her job was literally to drag me over the goal-line. And she did that exceedingly well. I'd like to thank others who shared their insights from their own book publishing experiences, and those included who where kind enough to "review" the book pre-publishing.

Thanks to my brother Jason, whose effortless swing is captured in each "Swing Thought." Jason hits a ball so far and high that one Scottish caddie was heard to say, "It'll come down when it gets hungry."

Recognition needs to go to the folks who took the photographs included herein. Several of my Pi Kappa Alpha fraternity brothers took shots from our Bandon Dunes golf trip. But special recognition goes to my brother-in-law Dr. Chad Gnam, who captured so many great moments on our Scotland golf trip, and a few from Sawgrass as well. This book would not have the life-giving energy of these photographs if Chad had not given so selflessly to chronicle these trips. I am most thankful to him, and all of my friends who lent a much-needed hand.

My brother-in-law, Chad, second shot, "The Alps," Prestwick Golf Club

# A Bucket of Balls

# A Bucket of Balls

As I do not play golf as frequently as I would like, I always try to start out on the practice range. Hitting a bucket of balls—chipping some and putting some. It helps bring back the feel and muscle memory.

When I don't have a chance to warm up before a round, I end up playing the first several holes poorly. I get frustrated, and then play the remaining holes even worse. Even if I finally do warm up, I have missed the opportunity to score well.

How often do we do the spiritual equivalent of waking up and going straight out onto the course without even one warm-up swing? Have you ever driven right out into 30 minutes of bumper-to-bumper traffic? Walked directly into a contentious negotiation? Or entered into a delicate discussion with a friend or loved one without saying a quick prayer?

What if that first interaction requires the equivalent of a strong drive? A driver is pretty hard to hit well with no preparation. What if the next moment requires the equivalent of a tight chip shot? Again, it's pretty tough to accomplish without any warm up at all.

I believe we run a tremendous risk on a daily basis when we go right into the important aspects of our lives without any preparation. I usually arrive at the golf course at least 45 minutes beforehand to warm up . . . so why don't we do the same in real life?

It is so important that we are prepared to take full advantage of the opportunities God puts before us each day. On the golf course, does it really matter if you miss-hit your first twelve shots? But in our daily interactions, God may be counting on us to provide a positive influence in someone else's life—to be His angels on earth.

## Swing Thought

Maybe we should start each day with a "bucket of balls" — quiet time, meditation, devotional reading, Bible reading or prayer . . . to be ready.

**Supporting Verses:**

*"Let the morning bring me word of your unfailing love, for I have put my trust in you. Show me the way I should go, for to you I entrust my life" (Psalm 143:8).*

*"Trust in the LORD with all your heart and lean not on your own understanding; in all your ways submit to him, and he will make your paths straight" (Proverbs 3:5-6).*

*"I came that they may have life, and have it abundantly"*

*(John 10:10).*

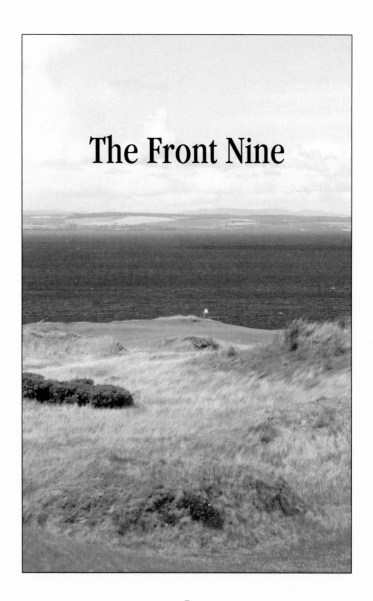

# The Front Nine

# The Front Nine

# ONE

# Position Yourself Correctly with the Ball

A good swing starts by putting our body into the correct relationship to the ball. For a longer shot, we usually set ourselves up so that the ball is toward the front of our stance. For a shorter shot, we align the ball more to the middle of our stance. For a chip shot, the ball may be a little back in our stance.

We do not walk up, take a stance, and then roll the ball where we want it to go. Instead, we address the ball exactly where it lies, and adjust our bodies to it accordingly. Not too close; not too far away. Not up ahead of it; not lagging behind. Even if we have to contort our bodies to create a shot out of the bushes, or deep in a sand trap, we do all we can to get our body into the best possible alignment with the ball—under the less-than-ideal circumstances.

We, as Christians, also should check our relationship to the circumstances in our lives, before we take the appropriate action. For example, when we have a friend in need—are we too close, invading their privacy with our own preconceived views? Or are we keeping our distance? Are we ahead of the situation or too far behind?

We need to approach each of our relational situations as we would in golf. We need to do all we can to get into the very best position possible, under the circumstances, to be an encouraging, positive influence.

But what if it is a particularly "tough shot?" A situation we have never experienced before, where we are required to get out of our comfort zone and act in a way we have never before acted?

Well, I have had to hit a ball left-handed with an upside down club before, where the ball was resting against a fence on the left side of the hole. I have sprayed mud all over myself when I have had to hit a ball out of shallow water. In fact, on the Western Gailes course in Scotland, I have a great series of pictures chronicling me "attempting" to hit out of a pot bunker on my knees!

Unfortunately, too often I have had to twist my body into a contorted stance to hit a shot. If I would not hesitate to attempt a strange shot out on the course, should I not feel as bold in real life—where it really matters?

## Swing Thought

How can I adjust my position so that I can meet the needs of others where they are? Do I need to get out of my comfort zone to do so?

**Supporting Verses:**

*"Be strong and courageous, and do the work. Do not be afraid or discouraged, for the LORD God, my God, is with you (1 Chronicles 28:20).*

*"I can do all things through him who strengthens me" (Philippians 4:13).*

*"For God is not a God of disorder but of peace . . ."*
*(I Corinthians 14:33).*

#17 "Road Hole," Old Course at St. Andrews

# TWO

# Find the Club that Fits You Best

Almost everyone who has played golf for a while probably has found that one particular club which is perfect for their individual stance and swing. More often than not when they hit with that club, they tend to hit a pretty good shot. Therefore, they develop a lot of confidence in that club.

For me, that club always has been my 4-iron. For whatever reason (actually, I think it is because I am 6' 3" but have always played with regular length clubs!), I hit that club pretty consistently (within the context of being an average golfer)—usually about 185 yards. In fact, a couple of summers ago, in typical "average golfer" fashion, when I was playing with my dad on a par 5, I topped my drive and did not make it to the fairway; hit a 185 yard 4-iron; hit another 185 4-iron; and tapped in for birdie!

I can use my 4-iron to gauge my 5-iron about 175 yards, my 6-iron 160 yards—you get the picture. I find it helpful to hit several shots on the practice tee with my

4-iron. And I often return to my 4-iron when my swing gets out of whack (which is often). It helps me regain my feel and rhythm . . . and confidence.

You may have a favorite Bible verse, hymn, prayer, thought, memory, or place of meditation. In this context, you have your "perfect club." The one upon which you can rely over and over again to regain your confidence, and to get your faith journey back on track.

If you do not have that "perfect club" yet—that perfect verse—keep an eye out for it. Intentionally seek it out through reading and prayer. It could be the key to improving, and maintaining, the momentum of your faith journey.

## Swing Thought

Rely upon, or develop, that one verse which speaks to you most directly. Then find more "favorite clubs."

**My Supporting Verse:**

*"Whatever you do, work at it with all your heart, as working for the Lord, not for human masters, since you know that you will receive an inheritance from the Lord as a reward. It is the Lord Christ you are serving"* *(Colossians 3:23-24).*

**Your Supporting Verse?:**

_____

_____

_____

_____

_____

_____

_____

*"Now faith is confidence in what we hope for and assurance about what we do not see"* *(Hebrews 11:1).*

#15, Kingsbarns Golf Links with a 4 iron

## THREE

# Swing Easy

One of the hardest "simple things" for me to accomplish in golf is to swing easy. Visualize with me for a moment that I am aimed correctly, balanced, and ready to hit my next shot. I think to myself, "keep my head down; keep my head down." The hole is 185 yards away, and I have a 4-iron in my hand—my perfect, confident 185 yard club. But it sure looks far away. So, in a moment of self-doubt, I lose faith in my swing and in my club. I take a bigger, faster swing, add some extra muscle, tighten my grip and . . . "kaboom" another bad shot into the lake, or into the woods, or bounding 100 yards in front of me.

I swing harder based fundamentally upon a lack of trust. It was a lack of trust in the club, which by the way is designed to hit the same yardage, every time. But there was also a lack of trust in my swing. I have heard teaching pros say over and over again, "Swing easy, and let the club do all the work."

Hmm. Let me ask you something. What if we substitute the words "Holy Spirit" for "club"? What would that mean in our lives? "Let the club do all the work." "Let the Holy Spirit do all the work."

God has anointed us all with the Holy Spirit. He is all around us and available to us to provide comfort, guidance, inspiration, healing, strength, love and peace. If we place our trust in the Holy Spirit, He will fill us with everything we need, when we need it.

## Swing Thought

**Swing easy, and let the "club" do all the work.**

**Supporting Verses:**

*"And I will ask the Father, and he will give you another advocate to help you and be with you forever—the Spirit of truth" (John 14:16-17).*

*"After they prayed, the place where they were meeting was shaken. And they were all filled with the Holy Spirit and spoke the word of God boldly" (Act 4:31).*

## FOUR

# Drive for Show;
# Putt for Dough

This is one of the great sayings in golf. I will confess that too often I focus on the big shots, on hitting the awesome 260 yard drives. In a typical 18-hole round, however, we only hit probably 14 drives, several of those possibly using a 3 wood. Average golfers usually don't hit very many 260 yard drives anyway— even when good contact is made.

Teeing off, hole #1,
Old Course at St. Andrews

But typically an average golfer will putt 36 times or more in a given round. And in addition, we will likely hit a lot of chip shots around the green. So if we are trying to play and score better, we need to focus on what is generally called "the short game." We have to remember that the short strokes count just as much as the big swings, and there are many more short strokes.

It's a command of the short game that makes someone a great golfer . . . and a great Christian servant. Jesus didn't win by pounding 400 yard drives to the astonishment of thousands of cheering admirers. The Gospels would read quite differently if His intent was to "shock and awe" the crowd!

Instead, He won by the equivalent of His "putting" touch and His "chipping" feel. He had the ability to read the slope of the green and to put the ball in the hole, every time, under every circumstance, with each person He met.

It's been stated that for the casual golfer, speed is more important than direction. Most of us have very

#18 TPC Sawgrass; perfect integration of speed and direction

low odds of sinking hard, long putts. That requires a perfect integration of speed and direction. Average golfers just don't play enough to develop that consistent ability. So, it's good advice to focus primarily on speed, to make sure that we get the ball close to the hole. Then, at worst, we are left with a short tap-in putt.

## Chapter Four

Along those lines, a few years ago a friend of mine from church left the teaching profession to pursue seminary training. He went on to become the pastor of a small church in rural Georgia. He shared that during his training, he had to complete a rotation providing spiritual care to patients at a hospital. He confessed that early on, he struggled with determining just the right thing to say to these patients, many of whom were facing significant medical challenges. Usually he had never met them before, so there was no prior relationship for him to draw upon. Ultimately, he shared with us the revelation that it was often the smallest gestures that had disproportionately positive impacts: merely saying hello, inquiring about how they were feeling that day, or even just sitting with them quietly in their rooms.

When we interact together, let's consider the important, positive effect that our "short game" can have on others. We don't always have to try to solve a problem with some profound observation or deep spiritual insight. Very often, we just have to be there for them or just "get it close."

## Swing Thought

Putt for dough.

**Supporting Verses:**

*"But when they arrest you, do not worry about what to say or how to say it. At that time you will be given what to say, for it will not be you speaking, but the Spirit of your Father speaking through you" (Matthew 10:19-20).*

*"In the same way, the Spirit helps us in our weakness. We do not know what we ought to pray for, but the Spirit himself intercedes for us through wordless groans" (Romans 8:26).*

# FIVE

# Consider the Elements

There are days when you are playing a course you know well, but it is windy—really windy. You can't hit

Bandon Dunes, 3 foursomes, nobody closest to the pin!

your driver, and your iron shots to the green come up short. You are being true to the fundamentals of your golf game, but the external forces are getting in the way of scoring well. We all get frustrated in these circumstances. More experienced golfers know that you have to take

the elements as they come . . . and adjust . . . and do the best you can. That being said, knowing and doing are two different things.

In 1998, with a business partner I launched a private equity fund in Atlanta to pursue buying smaller, established companies in the Southeast. We experienced significant, early success. In fact, over the next two and a half years we ultimately controlled over $120 million in growing revenue.

Then, beginning in 2000 one company after another started to experience their own, unique set of issues.

Many of these were tied to dramatic industry declines. Other issues surfaced from within the businesses. They kept coming at such a rapid pace that I remember almost laughing (probably to choke back the tears) at the unending, unbelievable nature and number of the issues. Needless to say, our fund was not successful, and six years of my business life ended with shutting down the fund.

That experience definitely counts as my "wind!" Yet, during that period, even though there were extreme periods of uncertainty—considering the elements—we did alright. We fought hard to protect our investments. We communicated the reality of the situation with our partners, and many of them remain friends. Our integrity helped us as we moved back into our prior professions. And, certainly for me, my faith and the strength of our family grew. So I think we did alright—considering the elements.

Are there inclement elements in your life affecting your play? Is your normal course—your normal life—playing tougher because of the life equivalents of wind, rain, hail, a tornado, or darkness? In those times, go back to your trusted clubs, trust in your swing, and mentally adjust your expectations as to how well you are doing ... considering the elements. It may be that God is using these circumstances to build your faith ... to draw you closer to Him.

## Chapter Five

## Swing Thought

Give yourself credit for how well you are doing— considering the elements.

**Supporting Verses:**

*"'For I know the plans I have for you,' declares the LORD, 'plans to prosper you and not to harm you, plans to give you hope and a future'" (Jeremiah 29:11).*

*"And we know that in all things God works for the good of those who love him, who have been called according to his purpose" (Romans 8:28).*

*"Not only so, but we also glory in our sufferings, because we know that suffering produces perseverance; perseverance, character; and character, hope. And hope does not put us to shame, because God's love has been poured out into our hearts through the Holy Spirit, who has been given to us" (Romans 5:3-5).*

*"Do not be anxious about anything, but in every situation, by prayer and petition, with thanksgiving, present your requests to God. And the peace of God, which transcends all understanding, will guard your hearts and your minds in Christ Jesus"* (Philippians 4:6-7).

SIX

# Etiquette

Out on the course, you can learn a lot about someone by how they treat the other players. How they handle adversity and triumph. How they respect the course. How they appreciate the opportunity to be playing golf in the first place.

Do they repair their divot on the green, and one more? Do they walk around the other player's putting line? Are they paying attention to their friends' shots?

In real life, how well do we treat each other? How do we handle adversity and triumph? How do we respect God's creation? Are we excited about having the chance to play? Are we grateful just to be invited out to the course? Or are we upset about the bad lie—self-centeredly walking through other's putting lines, hitting our own shots without waiting for our turn?

I have played golf with many whose attitudes, love and respect for the game have made the outing even more enjoyable. And I have played golf with a few folks whose insensitivity, discouragement or self-centeredness lessened the groups' enjoyment.

The etiquette rules of golf are designed to make play enjoyable for all—for you, the people in your group, and the people coming behind you. We are not on the course of life by ourselves or for ourselves; so how we act and what we do impacts everyone around us.

Jesus left us with simple instructions in this regard. "Here is a simple, rule-of-thumb guide for behavior: Ask yourself what you want people to do for you, then grab the initiative and do it for them. Add up God's Law and Prophets and this is what you get" (Matthew 7:12, The Message).

## Swing Thought

Consider how your small actions and interactions may make life richer for you and those around you.

## Chapter Six

**Supporting Verses:**

*"So in everything, do to others what you would have them do to you, for this sums up the Law and the Prophets" (Matthew 7:12).*

*"... set an example for the believers in speech, in conduct, in love, in faith and in purity" (1 Timothy 4:12).*

*"Do nothing out of selfish ambition or vain conceit. Rather, in humility value others above yourselves" (Philippians 2:3).*

*Preach the Gospel at all times, and when necessary, use words.* ~*St. Francis of Assisi*

Sahara bunker, #17, Prestwick Golf Club

## SEVEN

# Self-Enforcement

Golf is one of the few sports requiring a player to call penalties on oneself. Hit the ball out of bounds, it's a stroke and you have to hit it again from where you started. Hit it in the lake—take a stroke, and drop the ball from the spot you last saw it, no closer to the hole. Can't find your ball in the woods? Again, take a penalty. (Note: It doesn't say if you can't find any ball. I've gone into the woods and found 5 balls before—just none that were mine.)

So I lose my ball and give myself a penalty. Now, when I am by myself in the woods, how many times would my playing companion know if it was really my ball? Almost never. Golf is truly self-policing. If you want to roll your ball an inch to a better lie, go ahead . . . no one will see you. Kick it out from behind a tree. Be my guest. *Only you will know.* It won't affect the other players' scores. It will only affect your score at the end of the round.

The "end of the round"—now that is powerful for us Christians, don't you think? At the end of the round you could boastfully proclaim your score, but it would be wrong. Why do it? Why give up your integrity to avoid a brief period of frustration? Why show one less stroke—when your score probably is already high to begin with? Why lie to win a three dollar bet in a golf game, or to position yourself for a new business opportunity?

Jesus asks us to follow His example, to live in the Truth. In our human weakness, when we fall a little short, He asks us to confess, ask for forgiveness, and then accept the consequences . . . and God's grace . . . then move on.

However, under golf's rules, attesting to a false score at the end of the round results in DISQUALIFICATION. *Hmm.*

## Swing Thought

Do not let minor rule violations undermine your ability to influence those around you.

## Chapter Seven

**Supporting Verses:**

*"In the same way, let your light shine before others, that they may see your good deeds and glorify your Father in heaven" (Matthew 5:16).*

*"Do not let any unwholesome talk come out of your mouths, but only what is helpful for building others up according to their needs, that it may benefit those who listen" (Ephesians 4:29).*

*"Do not use dishonest standards when measuring length, weight or quantity. Use honest scales and honest weights, an honest ephah and an honest hin" (Leviticus 19:35-36).*

*"And what does the Lord require of you? To act justly and to love mercy and to walk humbly with your God"* *(Micah 6:8).*

## EIGHT

# Check Your Aim

For several years I hit my golf shots consistently to the right. I could see what was happening—it's pretty obvious when your shots keep ending up in the right rough, in the right trees, or even out of bounds on the right! I remember a particularly momentous shot from the tee box of the picturesque 18th hole at Harbour Town Golf Links in Hilton Head, South Carolina, where I fired my drive 260 yards dead to the right—easily clearing the five-story condominiums lining the hole!

To fix the problem I worked repeatedly on my ball position and my golf grip. I focused on my weight-shift and hip-turn. I pleaded with myself to keep my head down. I tried every swing thought I could. I even tried not to have any swing thoughts at all! Yet still I kept hitting to the right.

Then one day, a playing companion was standing right behind me on the tee-box as I set up to hit my driver. He said, "Dude, you are aimed dead right!" I immediately laid my club down on the ground parallel with my feet, stepped back behind where I had been standing, and what do you know, he was correct! The end of my driver shaft was pointing directly into the trees to the right.

The fact is, if your ball keeps ending up on the right, or the left, of the fairway—it may be because you are aiming there!

#3, Bandon Dunes

How can this awareness translate to us as Christians? First, it suggests that we should candidly evaluate the results of our actions. Are we happy most of the time? Thankful? At peace?

Or do we seem to find ourselves repeatedly feeling under pressure? Unbalanced? Guilty? Unfulfilled? Depressed?

Finding ourselves repeatedly "in the rough" in our lives may suggest that we need to move back from the situation, and assess where we are aiming our life. Are we aimed toward the wrong place, even as we struggle to try to play better? Are we surrounded by the wrong friends, in the wrong job, burdened by the wrong desires or concerns? All the while are we struggling daily with minor modifications in our life, hoping some simple act will get us back on track?

You might attend church and live a moral life, but if you continue to aim in the wrong direction—job-focused, money-focused, status-focused, self-focused—it should come as no surprise that your ball will continue to land in the rough.

## Swing Thought

Step back and look at your life. Are you truly aimed where God would have you go?

**Supporting Verses:**

*"Stand at the crossroads and look; ask for the ancient paths, ask where the good way is, and walk in it, and you will find rest for your souls" (Jeremiah 6:16).*

*"Let your eyes look straight ahead; fix your gaze directly before you. Give careful thought to the paths for your feet and be steadfast in all your ways. Do not turn to the right or the left; keep your foot from evil" (Proverbs 4:25-27).*

*"Have I not commanded you? Be strong and courageous. Do not be afraid; do not be discouraged, for the Lord your God will be with you wherever you go"* (Joshua 1:9).

# NINE

# The Round Is 18 Holes Long

Golf is not a single shot. It is not a single hole. It is 18 holes. Some short, some long; some hard, some easy. While each hole is a complete hole unto itself, it exists within a continuum of holes.

Our lives can be seen much like a golf course. It is a series of connected parts; but with each part a "hole" unto itself. You probably can envision your life as a Front Nine and a Back Nine. Can you remember some easy holes in your life? Some miraculous birdies!? Some pretty tough par-fives? Some embarrassing blow-up holes?

I find a lot of satisfaction in playing a good hole, and a lot of relief when a bad hole is over. And usually I have the same yearning for a good next hole. More importantly, for an enjoyable round.

Just as each golf course is different, so too is each life. You and I might be contemporaries, with similar jobs and similar life stages. Yet even if we teed off essentially at the same time, we may be playing very different courses. Yours might be manicured (it might be Augusta!); mine might be a devilish links course. You might be struggling on the number-one handicap hole—a monster, up-hill par four; and I might be playing an easy par three with a giant green and an inviting pin placement. I might be playing in a driving Scottish rain, and you may be hitting 50 yards further than usual in the clear altitude of Telluride, CO.

Thus, we cannot compare ourselves to each other, to each other's life courses, or to the elements affecting our respective play at the moment. We cannot grade ourselves too harshly against someone who has played 17 holes of their faith journey, when we might be just teeing off. We are each experiencing our own "course," with its own unique impact on our faith journey.

## Swing Thought

Consider with joy the rewards of your own spiritual journey, and make the most of your unique gifts.

**Supporting Verses:**

*"We have different gifts, according to the grace given to each of us. If your gift is prophesying, then prophesy in accordance with your faith; if it is serving, then serve; if it is teaching, then teach; if it is to encourage, then give encouragement; if it is giving, then give generously; if it is to lead, do it diligently; if it is to show mercy, do it cheerfully"* (Romans 12:6-8).

*"Now you are the body of Christ, and each one of you is a part of it. And God has placed in the church first of all apostles, second prophets, third teachers, then miracles, then gifts of healing, of helping, of guidance, and of different kinds of tongues. Are all apostles? Are all prophets? Are all teachers? Do all work miracles? Do all have gifts of healing? Do all speak in tongues? Do all interpret? Now eagerly desire the greater gifts"* (1 Corinthians 12:27-31).

*"Not so with you. Instead, whoever wants to become great among you must be your servant"* (Matthew 20:26).

# The Back Nine

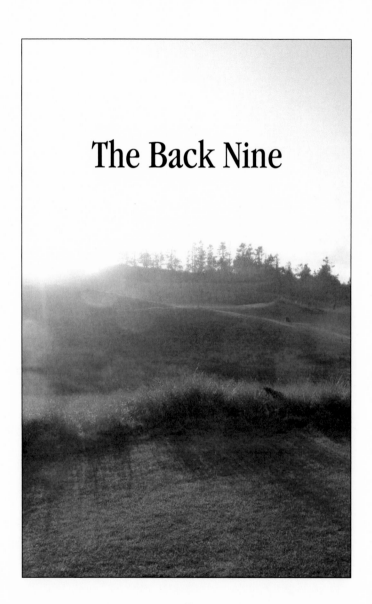

# The Back Nine

TEN

# Links Courses

Most American golfers play standard country club or municipal courses, which are usually laid out with nice fairways and well defined roughs. We are rewarded for the good shot and know exactly what to expect from our lie. In fact, the courses often are so well manicured that we can become annoyed when we find the ball on any imperfect lie, or when the ball takes a weird bounce and ends up in trouble unexpectedly.

Now, in Europe a common course style is called "links," and it is fundamentally the opposite. These courses are designed to conform to the land as it is, undulating, with harsh roughs and deep pot-bunkers. I recently had the chance-of-a-lifetime to play eight links courses in Scotland. For an average golfer, they were tough!

On a "links course," a great drive can careen right into a seven foot hole, where the only shot is to hit it out, sideways.

Western Gailes Golf Club;
no where to go but right

Reasonably well-hit balls curve along the fairway and roll into the rough, where if you are lucky, you take a giant swing with a 9-iron in tall grass and the ball may go 75 yards.

I do not know about you, but based upon my own life experience, I think God's creation is a lot more like a links course, than an American-style club course. Nevertheless, I'm afraid I often expect my life to unfold like a manicured Augusta. Our expectations are thus very important. How we react to a ball going into a pot bunker has a lot to do with whether we were expecting that possibility. It depends on whether we think it is "fair" for the pot bunker to be there in the middle of the fairway in the first place.

We should expect the unexpected. We need to view and expect our lives to be more like links courses. With this perspective, each situation is a challenge to see how well we handle it and move forward.

I am reminded of how our church service ended at my church growing up in Nashville, Tennessee. We would stand, hold hands, and sing, "Peace to you, peace to you, God's great peace to you. As you walk through your life, *enjoy your strife*, God's peace, God's peace to you."

## Chapter Ten

## Swing Thought

Try singing that sometime when you are in the "pot bunker."

**Supporting Verses:**

*"I have told you these things, so that in Me you may have peace. In this world you will have trouble. But take heart! I have overcome the world" (John 16:33).*

*"Rejoice always, pray continually, give thanks in all circumstances; for this is God's will for you in Christ Jesus" (1 Thessalonians 5:16-18).*

*"I waited patiently for the Lord; He turned to me and heard my cry. He lifted me out of the slimy pit, out of the mud and mire; He set my feet on a rock and gave me a firm place to stand. He put a new song in my mouth, a hymn of praise to our God. Many will see and fear the Lord and put their trust in Him" (Psalm 40:1).*

*"Dear children, let us not love with words or speech but with actions and in truth"* (I John 3:18).

Most demanding course we played in Scotland:
The Castle Course, St. Andrews

**ELEVEN**

# "Hit It Straight"

A partner with a private equity fund, who is also a fraternity brother of mine, shared with me the following story.

He was visiting China and had the opportunity to play a new golf course. As you might imagine, the rapid economic growth in China has led to a growing number of golf courses, yet at the time the game was still relatively new.

The foursome had a Chinese caddie assigned to them, a gentleman whose English was not the best, but who was clearly enthusiastic about the game. On one of the early holes, my friend stood on the tee-box, surveyed the hole, and realized the hole was a "dog-leg right."

My friend asked his caddie, "Where should I try to hit the ball?" The caddie answered in Chinese-accented English, and with a nodding head and a big smile, "Hit it straight!" They all chuckled at this response.

As the round continued, each time my friend asked the caddie where he should try to hit his shot, the caddie answered with the same big smile and nodding head, "Hit it straight!" This became the highlight of the round, and the foursome enjoyed anticipating the caddie's answer each time.

Now, to be candid, one of the hardest acts for any average golfer is actually to "hit it straight!" I do not hit the ball straight very often. Nevertheless, I often mentally analyze where to hit the ball for the "perfect" positioning. Frankly, I spend a lot of energy on the course envisioning a very elusive perfection.

My fraternity brother considered the caddie's consistent advice, "Hit it straight!" in a broader perspective. He wondered how often we over-think situations in our own lives. How often do we try to figure out exactly how we should approach a particular problem or relationship? Or we agonize over the perfect thing to say, or excessively analyze all of the possible ramifications for our actions?

Instead, maybe we should just follow the uncompli-cated advice of the Chinese caddie—"Hit it straight" and don't over-think each shot! We can trust God's Word to give us guidance in our daily decisions, and we can find direction through regular times of prayer.

## Chapter Eleven

## Swing Thought

Just "Hit it straight!"

**Supporting Verse:**

*"Jesus answered him . . . 'And you shall love the Lord your God with all your heart, with all your soul, with all your mind, and with all your strength.' This is the first commandment. And the second, like it, is this: 'You shall love your neighbor as yourself.' There is no other commandment greater than these"* (Mark 12:30-31).

*"Now listen, you who say, 'Today or tomorrow we will go to this or that city, spend a year there, carry on business and make money.' Why, you do not even know what will happen tomorrow. What is your life? You are a mist that appears for a little while and then vanishes. Instead, you ought to say, 'If it is the Lord's will, we will live and do this or that.'"* (James 4:13-15).

## TWELVE

# Clear Your Mind

Often we are told that, at the moment of the swing, we should clear our mind—and let the club do all the work. For average golfers, who are constantly working out kinks in their game, this can be tough to do! I usually have at least one of these swing thoughts—"just keep my head down," or "just swing easy," or "rotate my body," or "keep my right elbow tucked in."

Sometimes I have had more than one swing thought. I can tell you from experience that having a bunch of swing thoughts is not good. Instead, I know I need to "empty my head," and rely on the swing that has become instinctive to me, for better or worse. When I do this successfully, I usually hit the ball better and more consistently.

This concept carries a powerful and striking parallel to the instruction many people receive regarding our relationship with God.

In that relationship, many great teachers suggest that we don't pray to God only for the purpose of receiving all the help we or others need, and that we don't merely praise God consistently. Rather, our prayer time needs to create the silence necessary so that we can *hear* God's responses and know His calling for our lives. We have to empty our minds first, so that God may fill them up.

When we meditate on God's Word, He fills our minds with His truth. Psalm 4:4 (NASB) says to "meditate in your heart ... and be still." My wife meditates regularly on Psalm 46:10 with the following mantra: "Be still and know that I am God.   Be still and know that I am.   Be still and know.   Be still.   Be."

To advance as golfers, we have to clear our minds of swing thoughts. To advance our faith journey, we need to create the quiet time to just "be" with God.

In doing so, there is no telling what He may reveal.

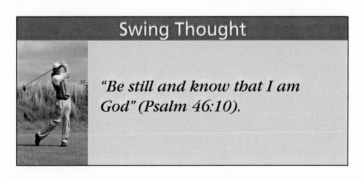

## Swing Thought

*"Be still and know that I am God" (Psalm 46:10).*

# THIRTEEN

# What's in the Bag?

The game of golf pits you, individually, against the course and the elements. All you have is your training, your natural ability, your swing, a bag of clubs, and the ball.

We have already identified the golf ball as that current situation we are addressing or reacting to as a Christian. We can see the comparison of the practice range to our time in prayer, in Bible study, and in service to others. We spoke also about the fact that the club can be seen as the Holy Spirit. Take a good, smooth swing, and let the "club" do all the work.

But what about the golf bag? Metaphorically, what role does it play in our lives? Consider for a moment the golf bag as the knowledge of God's Word, the Holy Bible.

Each unique club in the golf bag can be compared to the specific knowledge and power God shares with us through His Word. If you have to carry the ball over water that is 200 yards out—the bag has a 3-wood you can use. If you have to pitch over the sand trap and land the ball softly—the bag has a loft wedge. If you miss it and go in the trap—you have a sand wedge. The bag has whatever club you need. And you would never go out onto the course without your bag, would you? Of course not! You wouldn't have the tools to be able to hit the ball.

Have you ever hit the ball on the other side of the fairway on a wet day? You can't take the golf cart off the paths on a wet day. So inevitably, since you have no idea what shot you can play, you un-strap your bag, heave it over your shoulder, and walk across the fairway. Why? Because you don't know what the situation may require, so you have to bring the whole bag, with all of its clubs, to be prepared.

Contrast that with this scenario. If I'm lazy (and probably a little too confident in where the ball may lie), I pick out only a few clubs which I'm quite sure will do the job. But after I trudge across the soggy fairway, I discover I do not have the club I need. Then I have to trudge all the way back to the cart and all the way back to the ball again. Or worse, I go ahead and hit the shot using the wrong club—often with a bad result.

Do we have our full bag of God's Word with us every day? Can we call to mind the verses we need in most situations? Or do we consistently trudge across the fairway with only a couple of clubs—or with no clubs at all?

If we have a tough, confrontational meeting in the office that is the equivalent of hitting out of the sand —where is our sand wedge? Where is our Bible? When we have gotten ourselves in a little trouble and need to punch out safely from the trees to the fairway, where is our 4-iron? Where is that passage in the Bible that would help us? Just as all the clubs we need are in the bag, so too the Bible has all the aid and wisdom we need for every situation we face.

When we start out playing golf, we usually begin with a 9-iron, 7-iron, 3-iron, a driver and a putter. These are the basic clubs we learn to hit, since we don't have enough skill yet to master additional clubs. As we grow in our mastery of the game, we add new clubs, and ultimately we use a full set. It takes a lot of time and practice to learn to hit all of the clubs. And sometimes, there are clubs that we never really master.

Similarly, to be an effective Christian, we have to explore the full measure of the Truth that is in the Bible. Not only do we need to know what is in the Bible, but we also need to know how to apply those truths when we need them. Like learning the game of golf, learning what's in the Bible takes time.

## Swing Thought

Where is your Bible right now? Make it the equivalent of having your golf bag always in the trunk— ready for any opportunity to play!

**My Supporting Verse:**

*"In the beginning was the Word, and the Word was with God, and the Word was God" (John 1:1).*

*"All Scripture is God-breathed and is useful for teaching, rebuking, correcting and training in righteousness, so that the servant of God may be thoroughly equipped for every good work" (2 Timothy 3:16-17).*

## FOURTEEN

# The Mulligan

Were I better versed in golf lore, I would be able to discuss the historical origins of the "mulligan." But since I'm not, I will just introduce the mulligan as the opportunity to hit another drive off of the first tee box. Many friendly golf games start with players offering a mulligan, if needed, after your first drive. Having the opportunity to hit a second shot allows everyone the chance to start their round off under much better circumstances.

If you are like me, you make mistakes in your normal golf game. Sometimes little ones. Sometimes huge ones. And sometimes I really wish I could take that shot over again—take a mulligan—and eliminate the first attempt from my score.

Along those lines, when I consider the Bible I tend to view the Old Testament as being very legalistic. When the people of Israel were acting in a pleasing way, they gained God's favor. When they were acting in an unpleasing way, they received God's judgment. The religion was based fundamentally upon the law, and infractions were not overlooked. That's the equivalent of me hitting my first drive out of bounds and my friends saying, "Tough luck, buddy."

The New Testament strikes me as moving in a very different direction as God demonstrates through the life of His Son, Jesus Christ, the gift of His redemptive grace —His willingness to forgive us for our sins. God's grace is our mulligan.

## Swing Thought

God gives us mulligans every day, if we will accept His Grace.

**My Supporting Verse:**
*"For God so loved the world that He gave his only begotten Son, that whoever believes in Him shall not perish but have everlasting life" (John 3:16).*

**FIFTEEN**

# Where's Your Caddie?

How many professional golfers—people who make their living playing golf every day—go out and play alone in tournaments against their competitors? Think about it. Not one. Each and every professional golfer has a caddie. For many, it's a caddie that has known them personally for many years.

A valuable caddie is someone who has walked the course the night before. It is someone who carefully watches where the ball lands and reads the golfer's distances. A faith-ful caddie carries their heavy bag for the long, hot summer rounds. It is someone who knows their in-ner feelings, how their mind works.
A loyal caddie knows how to settle down the golfer when he or she gets anxious, and how to get them excited when they need to make a charge. Dedicated

caddies look over their shoulder, read every putting line, and fix their divots after each shot.

Professional players *don't go it alone.* They rely heavily—*heavily*—on their caddies.

As Christians, we have a personal relationship with God, our heavenly Father, with Jesus, our Savior, and with the Holy Spirit, our Counselor and Comforter. We can rely heavily on all three because the Father, Son and Holy Spirit know each of us better than we know ourselves. Furthermore, they are always present to guide us into all truth.

## Swing Thought

We are never alone on the course of life.

## Chapter Fifteen

**Supporting Verses:**

*"But the Counselor, the Holy Spirit, whom the Father will send in my name, will teach you all things and will remind you of everything I have said to you" (John 14:26).*

*"I have been crucified with Christ and I no longer live, but Christ lives in me. The life I now live in the body, I live by faith in the Son of God, who loved me and gave himself for me" (Galatians 2:20).*

P.S. In an interesting side note, professional golfers often share 10 percent of their winnings with their caddie. See any parallel to "tithing?"

*"Do nothing out of selfish ambition or vain conceit. Rather, in humility value others above yourselves"* (Philippians 2:3).

# SIXTEEN

# Sharing the Joy of the Game

Let me ask you a question. How were you introduced to the game of golf? Did your father or mother play? Did you drive the golf cart with them when you were young? Did a friend invite you out on the course for the first time, and lend you a set of golf clubs? Were you self-motivated by watching a golf tournament on television, and did you say to yourself, "Hey, I could do that!"?

Were you intrigued by how deeply people enjoyed the game, no matter what their proficiency level? Or were you fascinated with how important making time for golf was in their lives? In one way or another, you were introduced to the game of golf. And then you played and played again until you were hooked! And then you wanted to make the game of golf an important part of your life.

Let me suggest that the many ways we come to golf are similar to the ways we are introduced to our faith. Our minister once pointed out that religion is, for the most part, inherited. At first, we tend to accept the faith or the denominational affiliation of our family. Maybe one of our family members sets an example for us, and we emulate their actions. Or possibly we may find our faith later in life. A friend may ask us to visit their church, or we may watch a pastor on television, or listen to a sermon on the radio, or read an intriguing book which caused us to decide to explore religion for ourselves. Inevitably our faith journey starts with some form of an introduction.

In your own life, you may have invited friends or business colleagues out to play golf. What better way to invest in a relationship than to show that their companionship is worth a few hours of your time?

Now, consider for a moment ways you might introduce this person to your faith. Have you invited someone to your church service, small group or church retreat? Recently? Ever? Have you invested several hours of quality time to get to know them better on a personal level, to have a shared experience or to discuss and compare your faith journeys? Consider whether there is someone who needs to be "introduced" to the Christian faith . . . by you.

## Swing Thought

Introduce your faith to one other person. Repeat.

**Supporting Verses:**

*"And He said to them, 'Follow Me, and I will make you fishers of men' (Matthew 4:19).*

*"Then He said to his disciples, 'The harvest is plentiful but the workers are few. Ask the Lord of the harvest, therefore, to send out workers into his harvest field'" (Matthew 9:38).*

*"Therefore, go and make disciples of all nations, baptizing them in the name of the Father and of the Son and of the Holy Spirit, and teaching them to obey everything I have commanded you. And surely I am with you always, to the very end of the age" (Matthew 28:19-20).*

*"Do not wear yourself out to get rich; do not trust your own cleverness. Cast but a glance at riches, and they are gone, for they will surely sprout wings and fly off to the sky like an eagle"*

*(Proverbs 23:4-5).*

Prestwick Golf Club

**SEVENTEEN**

# Where Do Great Shots Come From?

One of the occurrences which keeps me longing to play golf over and over again is hitting the "great shot." Now, professional golfers hit a lot of great shots. *Really* great shots ... most of the time. In fact, when they don't hit a great shot, I expect they are pretty disappointed. And, to be honest, when I don't hit a great shot, I am disappointed too. But only a little bit because I know I am an average golfer. When I get the ball on the green from 150 yards, I'm happy—anywhere on the green.

But I am truly elated when I set up correctly over the ball, clear my mind, take a nice, easy swing, trust the club to do the work, and hit a beautiful, arching 185-yard shot with my 4-iron right into the middle of the green—an ELEVATED GREEN, PROTECTED BY SAND TRAPS ... OVER A LAKE. Doesn't that make the visual image even sweeter! Anyone who has

Nephew Jack, #17, TPC Sawgrass

played golf, or even watched golf, knows the pure satisfaction that accompanies a "great shot."

So, one might ask, how do average golfers hit great shots? If they are average, why aren't they content to just hit "average" shots? And then when they become pros, they can strive to hit "great shots!"

The fact is that each of us—the beginning golfer, the average golfer, the pro golfer—all possess the same inherent ability to hit the great shot. Some with more frequency than others, for sure, but all of us have an equal ability to hit the great shot.

Why? Because we are all connected and governed by the same laws of physics, by the same equipment and the same course layouts.

The same physical forces which allow the top pro golfers to hit drives averaging over 300 yards, also allow you and me to hit an amazing drive. The same physical forces which allow Phil Mickelson to hit his fabled "flop shot," allow you and me to hit an amazing flop shot. The same physical and gravitational forces that enable the pros to correctly read and sink a 40-foot putt with a huge sweeping break also allow us "average golfers" to do the same.

In fact, often we can read an article regarding the mechanics of a particular shot, go out, and with some practice closely replicate that shot. The powerful point here is that the professional golfers don't access a DIFFERENT set of rules, physics or forces that enable them to hit great shots—they access the same forces as you and I.

The difference is their commitment, their study, their practice, their access to great teachers, their willingness to harness those forces and influences and apply them relentlessly over a long period of time to develop a professional level game—and probably a good measure of God-given talent. When they hit a great shot, they merely represent the ever-present "potential" inherent in each and every one of us.

So they are not different from us, they are not separate from us. They are a "progression" of us. They were all once average golfers. They have developed and now represent the embodiment of our own golfing potential.

The connection here is simply this: as believers, we are all the children of God. He is the Father of each of us. And everybody on earth has the same opportunity to enjoy a direct, intimate relationship with Him. In that relationship, we have access to all of God's peace, all of His grace and all of the gifts and talents He has placed or will place into our lives. We all have been left by Jesus with the witness of His life, with His offer of salvation and with the Holy Spirit. Through prayer, meditation on His Word and submission to His will, we all share this "equal access."

While many of them clearly are advanced in their faith journeys, I don't believe that God saves some special knowledge, insight, or exclusive revelation for the senior pastors, recognized religious book authors, or the missionaries of the world; or any particular group or denomination.

I am suggesting that we have the same access to His grace and peace and wisdom and power as any of those who we may perceive as being a little more spiritually advanced on their faith journey—in the golf context, the "pros." But just as we can all hit "great shots" and just as we all can improve our golf scores through focus, repetition and learning, so too can each of us move from being "average Christians" to being "exceptional Christians."

Our family has been inspired by this quote from Marianne Williamson:

> *"Our deepest fear is not that we are inadequate. Our deepest fear is that we are powerful beyond measure. It is our light, not our darkness that most frightens us. We ask ourselves, Who am I to be brilliant,*

*gorgeous, talented, fabulous? Actually, who are you not to be? You are a child of God. Your playing small does not serve the world. There is nothing enlightened about shrinking so that other people won't feel insecure around you. We are all meant to shine, as children do. We were born to make manifest the glory of God that is within us. It's not just in some of us; it's in everyone. And as we let our own light shine, we unconsciously give other people permission to do the same. As we are liberated from our own fear, our presence automatically liberates others."*

## Swing Thought

You are fearfully and
wonderfully made.

**Supporting Verses:**

*"I thank You because I am fearfully and wonderfully made" (Psalm 139:14)*

*"… for assuredly I say to you, if you have the faith as a mustard seed, you will say to this mountain, 'Move from here to there,' and it will move; and nothing will be impossible for you" (Matthew 17:20).*

*"After this the Lord appointed seventy-two others and sent them two by two ahead of Him to every town and place where He was about to go … The seventy-two returned with joy and said, "Lord, even the demons submitted to us in Your name" (Luke 10:1; 10:17).*

## EIGHTEEN

# God Relies on "Average Golfers"

Throughout the Old and New Testament, it seems to me that God has consistently turned to His more "average" golfers to lead His people. Moses was an abandoned child and a poor public speaker, yet by trusting God, Moses led God's people out of bondage.

David was a small boy, who made one of the "great shots" in history against Goliath! Matthew was a tax collector. Peter, who followed God's vision and led the cause of evangelism to the Gentiles, was a fisherman. And Paul, who pursued the persecution of early disciples and who God had to blind for three days just to get his attention, came from a family of tent-makers!

Mary and Joseph could not have been more "average," and yet through the Holy Spirit they brought Jesus into the world and raised Him through His formative years. Even Jesus was a carpenter until He began His ministry.

Throughout the ages there have been many great rulers, many great prophets, many great religious scholars and many great warriors. And yet, as we read through the Bible, God seems to consistently call upon and rely upon His "average golfers" to advance His will, to be His hands and heart here on earth. Through His grace, He has taken those average golfers and transformed them into exceptional professionals!

## Swing Thought

Remember, the 12 disciples were pretty average and yet, 2000 years later ... quite a legacy.

**Supporting Verses:**

*"When they saw the courage of Peter and John, and realized that they were unschooled, ordinary men, they were astonished and they took note that these men had been with Jesus" (Acts 4:13).*

*"I am the vine, you are the branches. He who abides in Me, and I in him, bears much fruit; for without Me you can do nothing" (John 15:5).*

*"Therefore, if anyone is in Christ, he is a new creation; the old has gone, the new has come" (2 Corinthians 5:17)!*

# The 19th Hole

*Golf is not a game
designed to be played
alone. It is not designed to
be celebrated alone—
nor tinkered with alone—
nor advanced alone.*

## NINETEEN

# The 19th Hole

Obviously there are 18 holes on a course, so the "19th hole" is the traditional name of the club bar, where golfers throughout the ages have reflected on their round, reveled in the highlights, poked fun at the more humorous shot outcomes, consoled the frustrated, celebrated the love of the game, and most probably had a beer.

In the context of our shared faith journey, consider this chapter as this book's "19th Hole." Take a moment to reflect on whether any of the thoughts or observations herein struck a chord within you. Are there any actions or steps you believe may be helpful to "improve your game?"

And further consider, in the spirit of the "19th hole," the value of sitting with your friends and discussing together your "game"—your current faith journey, as well as their own.

I made a comment to my brother-in-law years ago while we were playing golf that I believe holds true for most average golfers. I speculated that golf was designed to be played in foursomes, because most average golfers don't hit enough good shots to make the round nearly as enjoyable as the combined good shots of a group of four. Like many people, I get as much enjoyment from watching a fellow player hit a great shot as I do hitting one myself.

Golf is not a game designed to be played alone. It is not designed to be celebrated alone—nor tinkered with alone—nor advanced alone. It takes a friend to tell you that you are aimed into the woods. It takes a friend to remind you to swing easy. It takes a friend to help you get over the bad hole.

Much like golf, I believe our faith walk also is pursued best with a "foursome," with close friends. We celebrate, commiserate and grow together.

Fraternity brothers, 19th hole, Bandon Dunes

## Chapter Nineteen

I have heard repeatedly and consistently from many mentors, who seem well along in their faith journey, that the most important act a guy can take is to meet regularly with a group of other men to share our faith journey together. I have had that opportunity to bond with other strong Christian men—and it has been one of the greatest blessings of my life.

## Swing Thought

Find an opportunity to bond with a few fellow faith travelers.

**My Supporting Verse:**

*"For where two or three are gathered together in My name, I am there in the midst of them" (Matthew 18:20).*

*"Bear one another's burdens, and so fulfill the law of Christ" (Galatians 6:2).*

*"How good and pleasant it is when God's people live together in unity" (Psalm 133:1)!*

*"Finally, brothers and sisters, whatever is true, whatever is noble, whatever is right, whatever is pure, whatever is lovely, whatever is admirable—if anything is excellent or praiseworthy—think about such things"* (Philippians 4:8).

Old Course at St. Andrews

## ABOUT THE AUTHOR

# David M. Felts

For over 25 years since college, David Felts has worked professionally in investment banking and private equity. He has lived in New York, Chicago, and then Atlanta. He has had an opportunity to work side by side with many successful business owners and executives.

While certainly an "average golfer," David has had the opportunity to play many great golf courses he never thought he would. And while certainly an "average Christian," David has benefited from the insights and encouragement of many strong Christians . . . in business, church, other ministries and most especially through his involvement in the Souly Business men's retreat ministry.

David is convinced that God is on the move during this present time. Especially with men—business men in particular—he sees the huge impact on businesses, employees, and families as more and more men see faith and work as pieces of the same whole, versus completely separate parts of life.

David grew up in Nashville, Tennessee and his education includes Montgomery Bell Academy; McIntire School of Commerce, The University of Virginia; and The J.L. Kellogg Graduate School of Management, Northwestern University. He lives in Atlanta, Georgia with his wife Jill, where they have raised two daughters.

*Swing Thoughts* is his first book.

*"I believe one of the next great moves of God is going to be through the believers in the workplace."* ~Billy Graham

# Resources

Other inspirational resources for renewing the mind and remembering to lean in on God:

**Compelling Creations** inspiration faith jewelry provides tangible cues to renew the mind and spirit daily. Each piece is handcrafted with a message that helps us strive to inspire, challenge, and uplift one another. *www.compelling-creations.com*

**Music to Light the World** offers God's peace, rest, hope and healing through the scripture-inspired piano of Stanton Lanier. The soothing and uplifting instrumentals supply a beautiful soundtrack for reading, prayer and daily life. *www.MusictoLighttheWorld.org*

Thank you for reading *Swing Thoughts.*
Share your story of how this book
has encouraged you in your faith journey—
or your golf game.

Visit *www.swingthoughtsbook.com,*
or email author David M. Felts at
*david@swingthoughtsbook.com*

Until we meet again.